the Charterhouse

THE GUIDEBOOK

g

the Charterhouse
in association with D Giles Limited, London

First published in 2016 by GILES
An imprint of D Giles Limited
4 Crescent Stables, 139 Upper Richmond Road,
London SW15 2TN, UK
www.gilesltd.com

A catalogue record for this book is available from the British Library

ISBN: 978-1-907804-97-7

This publication marks the completion of the 'Revealing the
Charterhouse' project which has been generously funded by the
Heritage Lottery Fund and several other charitable trusts.

For the Charterhouse:

Text: Dr Cathy Ross

Design: Joe Ewart for Society

Production Editor: Tom Hobson

Photography: Tom Hobson, Emma Morris and others

Thanks are due to Dr Stephen Porter and Dominic Tickell for
historical advice and overseeing the content

For D Giles Limited:

Proof-read by David Rose

Produced by GILES, an imprint of D Giles Limited, London

Printed and bound in China

Contents

Foreword   5

the Charterhouse   7

the Museum   13

the Tour   42

the Square   58

Visitor Information   62

'I went under an arch ...
it was like moving into the
Fourth Dimension, several
centuries back in Time,
everything round about
completely still, like a dream.'

Anthony Powell, 1985

Foreword

I am delighted to welcome you to the Charterhouse and hope you enjoy your visit. The Charterhouse has played a part in many lives over the last 650 years but, although many have known of the place, few have ventured inside. The "Revealing the Charterhouse" project is an important departure as, for the first time, we are opening our gates to visitors so that you can experience the rich history embedded in this remarkable place.

The Charterhouse has one core purpose which is to offer a community for elderly people in financial and social need. More than 40 Brothers, as we call them, make their home here. We provide for our Brothers to live independent, purposeful lives in the modern world, guided by the spirit of hospitality of our founder, Thomas Sutton. However we also know that the Charterhouse has been witness to many of the events that have shaped our nation's history. We are grateful to the Heritage Lottery Fund and many other donors for enabling us to share this history through our new museum, learning centre and, not least, the gardens in Charterhouse Square, now open to the public for the first time.

The Charterhouse has been 'living the nation's history since 1348'. You are most welcome to explore the rich history of the Charterhouse.

Brigadier Charlie Hobson OBE
Master of the Charterhouse

the Charterhouse

The Charterhouse is one of London's great survivals. The place is called the Charterhouse after the English name for a monastery of the Carthusian order – which is how the buildings began. In 1371, a religious community was established here, on the site of a Black Death burial ground which was opened in 1348. Over the centuries, the Charterhouse became one of the great aristocratic houses of Tudor London; and then, Europe's most well-endowed charity.

Today, the Charterhouse remains a charitable foundation although no longer Europe's largest. The long form of the charity's name is 'Sutton's Hospital in Charterhouse', after the founder Thomas Sutton (1532–1611). Sutton was a self-made man whose shrewd business dealings in late Tudor England made him into England's wealthiest commoner. He was also a philanthropist who used his wealth to found a school for the young and an almshouse for the old.

Today, both institutions are flourishing. Charterhouse School has moved out of London, but the original site continues to provide sheltered accommodation to a group of pensioners, known as the Brothers of the Charterhouse. Today's Brothers live here by virtue of Thomas Sutton's decision to use his wealth to do good.

The Brothers and Thomas Sutton are not the only characters in Charterhouse's history. Thousands of other lives have been caught up with this site. Monks, bishops, kings, queens, dukes, earls, servants, merchants, nurses, schoolboys and pensioners all people Charterhouse's rich past. Many lived here, others worked here, some are buried here. Every generation has added something new. And all have left their mark.

Thomas Sutton's Coat of Arms

Thomas Sutton's coat of arms can be seen throughout the Charterhouse. It was adopted by Sutton's Hospital as a reminder of the charity's founder. The full coat of arms includes a greyhound crest and the motto *Deo Dedi Dante* (because God has given, I give).

the Timeline

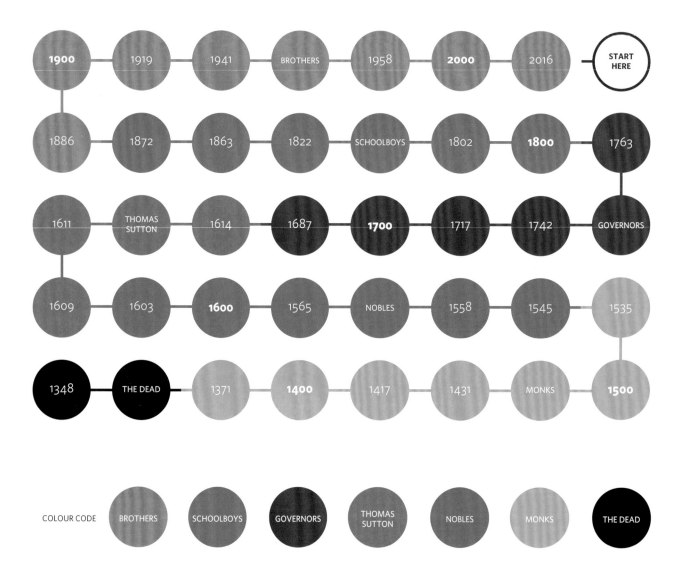

1900	1919	1941	BROTHERS	1958	**2000**	2016	START HERE
1886	1872	1863	1822	SCHOOLBOYS	1802	**1800**	1763
1611	THOMAS SUTTON	1614	1687	**1700**	1717	1742	GOVERNORS
1609	1603	**1600**	1565	NOBLES	1558	1545	1535
1348	THE DEAD	1371	**1400**	1417	1431	MONKS	**1500**

COLOUR CODE   BROTHERS   SCHOOLBOYS   GOVERNORS   THOMAS SUTTON   NOBLES   MONKS   THE DEAD

YEAR	EVENT
2016	The Charterhouse opens its gates to visitors
2000	
1958	Visit of Queen Elizabeth II, to formally open the restored Charterhouse buildings
1941	In May 1941, a direct hit by an incendiary bomb causes a devastating fire. The Brothers are evacuated
1919	The Brothers no longer have to wear a black cloak in public
1900	
1886	A Parliamentary Bill proposing that the historic buildings are demolished is withdrawn
1872	Charterhouse School moves to Godalming. Merchant Taylors' School buys the vacated site for £90,000
1863	Charterhouse School is present at the first meeting of the Football Association
1822	William Makepeace Thackeray joins the school, aged 11
1802	A new school building is erected on the site of the former Great Cloister
1800	
1763	Governors begin to develop their Clerkenwell estate north of the hospital
1742	Governors support the enclosure of Charterhouse Square, which becomes a fashionable London address
1717	Elizabeth Holford bequeaths £4,700 to provide university scholarships for the schoolboys
1700	
1687	The staunchly Protestant governors defy James II's request to admit a Catholic as a Brother

YEAR	EVENT
1614	Sutton's Hospital opens, admitting the first Scholars and Poor Brothers
1611	Thomas Sutton establishes his charitable foundation a few months before his death. His executors begin transforming Howard House into Sutton's Hospital
1609	Thomas Sutton petitions Parliament for leave to establish his charity
1603	King James I holds his first court at Howard House by invitation of its owner, the Earl of Suffolk
1600	
1565	The fourth Duke of Norfolk buys the Charterhouse. He renames the main building Howard House
1558	Queen Elizabeth I stays at the Charterhouse for four days on the eve of her formal entry into the City of London
1545	The site is bought by Sir Edward North who remodels the ruined buildings as a courtyard house
1535	Prior John Houghton is executed for treason. Subsequently, the monastery is closed and the buildings seized by the Crown
1500	
1430–31	A system of pipes brings fresh water from springs at Islington into the monastery
1417	The building of the Great Cloister is completed
1400	
1371	A Carthusian monastery, The House of the Salutation of the Mother of God, is founded at Smithfield by Sir Walter Manny and the Bishop of London
1348	Outbreak of the Black Death. Two burial grounds open at Smithfield

A DAY IN THE LIFE OF THE CHARTERHOUSE

7:00 AM	The Night Porter opens the gates and the main doors
7:55	Bell rings for Chapel service
8:15–9:00	Breakfast cooked and served for the Brothers. Gardeners and building staff arrive
9:00–12:00	Office staff and volunteers arrive. Morning activities include: gardening, office work, cleaning, nursing work in the Infirmary. Some Brothers undertake voluntary work, read newspapers in the Library or go shopping
11:00	The shop, museum and the Square's gardens open to the public
12:00	A group of Brothers go to the pub before lunch (three times a week)
12:55 PM	Bell rings for 1:00 Lunch in the Great Hall
2:00–4:00	Various activities: some Brothers lead guided tours around the Charterhouse
3:45	Brothers' tea in the Great Hall
5:00	End of public opening hours. Day Staff leave
5:30	Evening prayers in the Chapel (open to the public)
6:30–7:30	Buffet supper for the Brothers in the Great Hall
7:00–10:30	Various activities: Brothers Book Club (once a month). Guests arrive for evening lectures, concerts or receptions in the Great Chamber
10:30	When all guests have left, the Night Porter locks the main doors and the Square gates

the Museum

The museum room at the Charterhouse is devoted to the people most associated with the Charterhouse over the centuries: Brothers, schoolboys, governors, Thomas Sutton, Tudor nobles and medieval monks. The museum ends with a victim of the Black Death, one of many Londoners who were buried on the site in 1348-9 and could be said to be the Charterhouse's oldest residents.

The room housing the museum has seen many changes over the centuries. Most recently it was a meeting room, archive store and billiard room for the Brothers. Before that it was Brooke Hall, the staffroom for Charterhouse School. Before 1611, the space was a passageway in the Tudor mansion – possibly a bowling alley. Before 1538, it had been part of the Great Cloister of the Carthusian monastery.

The history of adaption and reuse is a Charterhouse characteristic. Today the buildings in the precinct feel ancient and venerable. Yet much of what visitors see is the work of architects John Seely and Paul Paget who were commissioned after the Second World War to restore Charterhouse's bomb-damaged buildings.

Seely and Paget aimed to reinstate the look and feel of Charterhouse, as it had stood before 1939 – an understandable goal in the immediate aftermath of the war. In realising this aim they enhanced the site's Tudor character but demolished some of the Victorian buildings in the interests of 'eliminating nineteenth-century alterations and distortions'. Charterhouse, as you see it today, incorporates the taste of the twentieth century, just as much as the taste of the Tudors.

An ancient chair

This chair has been at the Charterhouse for many years, but no one can say quite how old it is. It has been much repaired over the years and incorporates wood of different ages.

A stone wall in Master's Court

Detail of a wall in Master's Court, showing a mix of building fabrics including medieval carved stone and Tudor bricks.

the Brothers

The Charterhouse today is home to the Brothers, a group of elderly gentlemen who live here thanks to the charitable actions of Thomas Sutton 400 years ago. Since 1614, when the first Brothers were admitted, many thousands of men have lived out their final years at the Charterhouse.

Admittance to the Charterhouse has always been conditional on needy circumstances and good behaviour. Past Brothers have all been needy, but not all have been well-behaved.

Originally, the hospital required the 'Poor Brothers', as they were first called, to be visible symbols of Protestant sobriety. They had to attend chapel daily, and pay a fine if they didn't turn up. Brothers also had to wear a uniform of black cloak and top hat when out in public. These rules were loosened in the early twentieth century.

Today's Brothers include men from a variety of backgrounds, with an even greater variety of personalities. They live in individual flats but share mealtimes together and have many common interests. There is an on-site Infirmary, an art studio, library and common room. Attendance at the regular chapel services is no longer compulsory. Several Brothers undertake voluntary work, both within and beyond the precinct. The Charterhouse provides sheltered accommodation with the added value of living in a community of independence, support and companionship.

The Old Charterhouse, 1964

Lithograph by Edward Ardizzone (1900–1979)

Ardizzone made two Charterhouse-related prints in the 1960s. The figures of the pensioners and the ancient mulberry tree, a survivor of wartime bombs, convey a mood of quiet but determined survival.

A Rainy Day, 1970s

Watercolour by Harold Hookway Cowles (1896–1987)

Harold Cowles became a Brother of the Charterhouse in 1970 following a career as an artist and illustrator. He was remembered by his friends as 'a steady and gentle sort of man'.

Welcome to the Blue Badge guides, 2005

Drawing by Syd Cain (1918–2011)

Syd Cain became a Brother after a career as a production designer in the film industry. His work in the 1960s and 1970s included the early James Bond films, for which he designed several of 007's gadgets. Whilst at the Charterhouse he drew many cartoons of life as a Brother. This example captured an incident when a speeding Syd scattered a tour group.

Messiaen: Eclairs sur l'Au-delà.   R. 1997

Messiaen: Eclairs sur l'Au-delà, 1997

Collage by Patrick Rowe (1917–2012)

Patrick Rowe was a professional artist who became a Brother of the Charterhouse in 2002. The titles of his collages reflected his musical interests but had no direct bearing on the artworks, which were 'merely decorations to delight the eye, it is as simple as that.'

During his time as a Brother, Patrick Rowe worked behind the counter at an artists' materials shop in Islington. He was well known to the customers and much missed on his death.

PAST BROTHERS

Early Brothers were described as 'decayed gentlemen, old soldiers, and ancient serving-men'. By the 1860s, 'respectable tradesmen' were being admitted and the body of Brothers included estate agents, publishers, wine merchants and a professor of mathematics. Past Brothers include:

Tobias Hume (d.1645)	Musician	A professional soldier, who also composed for the *viola da gamba*.
John Bagford (d.1716)	Book collector	A collector of rare broadsides, now known as *The Bagford Ballads*.
Elkanah Settle (d.1724)	Poet	A political poet who sold verses in Bartholomew Fair dressed as a dragon in a green leather suit.
Stephen Gray (d.1736)	Scientist	A pioneer in the field of electricity who explored induction and conductivity through a series of experiments, some made at the Charterhouse.
John Barlow (d.1814)	Artist	An engraver who made prints for William Hogarth and William Blake.
Thomas Stothard (d.1834)	Artist	An artist, engraver and Royal Academician. Two of his sons also became Brothers.
W.T. Moncrieff (d.1857)	Dramatist	A theatrical Impresario who wrote and produced spectacular shows. He entered the Charterhouse when he lost his sight.
Andrew Chatto (d.1864)	Writer	An editor, writer and magazine publisher, formerly a tea dealer from Newcastle upon Tyne.
John Maddison Morton (d.1891)	Dramatist	Writer of comic farces including *My First Fit of Gout* and his smash hit, *Box and Cox*.
Walter Greaves (d.1930)	Artist	Son of a boatbuilder who became a painter of river scenes. On entering the Charterhouse his hair went white overnight (he stopped using hair dye).

The school football team, 1862

Pictured outside the Norfolk Cloister, where boys played 'cloister football' and invented the offside rule.

Henry Herschel Hay Cameron of Charterhouse, 1864

Photographed aged 12 by his mother, Julia Margaret Cameron, who included her son's school in the title of his portrait. H.H. Cameron was a member of the Epicure Club and contributed the small sketch shown below to the club's minute book.

the Schoolboys

The first schoolboys at the Charterhouse were the 40 Foundation Scholars who arrived in 1614, their education, board and lodging to be provided free thanks to Thomas Sutton. By the time Charterhouse School moved out of London in 1872, the institution had grown and was now taking fee-paying dayboys ('Oppidans') and boarders alongside the Foundation Scholars ('Gownboys'). The school occupied the lion's share of the site, using the former monastic Great Cloister for its grounds.

Boys could have very different experiences at Charterhouse School. Pupils were often left to fend for themselves, establishing their own codes of conduct, rituals, games and punishments. Many boys thrived in the freedom and camaraderie this generated. Others found it hard. One former pupil remembered it as '... *the end of a cruel age for children and I should not like to go through it again. The rareness of interference from above left us to choose for ourselves good or evil, work or idleness: it strengthened the strong, if it did not shelter the weak.*' (L.R. Phelps).

The tendency to invent-your-own-rules had happy results for the game of football. The offside rule is said to have originated at Charterhouse School to cope with the particular issues of playing indoor football in the long and thin Norfolk Cloister. The School was among the pioneers of the modern game, attending the first meeting of the Football Association in 1863. In 1881, a team of 'Old Carthusians' won the English FA Challenge Cup , the last amateur club to do so.

Page from the Epicure Club minute book, 1864

This club was one of several formed at Charterhouse School by groups of friends. Epicure Club members gave themselves silly names ('The Great Grumbo') and put on concerts.

William Makepeace Thackeray's doodles, 1822–8

Thackeray grew up to become a famous novelist and one of Charterhouse School's most celebrated old boys. These doodles were 'done by him when at Charterhouse'. He didn't enjoy his schooldays, later describing the Charterhouse as 'the Slaughter House School, near Smithfield'.

Schoolboy graffiti

Carved into a pew in the schooboys' bay of the Chapel, added in 1825.

A DAY IN THE LIFE OF A FAG, 1870

Fagging, whereby younger boys ('petties') acted as servants to the older boys ('uppers'), was common but not necessarily a source of unhappiness as it could protect against bullying.

7:00 AM	Hurries to wake his 'upper' (fag-master)
7:00–7:40	Washes in cold water; fetches hot water for his upper, cleans his basin and sees that his towels are dry
8:00–8:30	First School
8:30 AM	Breakfast (roll and butter with a pint of tea). Slices and toasts the roll for his upper; makes his tea or coffee
9:30–12:00	School. Before dinner a fag may be conscripted for racket-fagging (sports activities)
1:00 PM	Dinner (meat and vegetables, with pudding three times a week)
2:00–5:00	School: on half-holidays the fag cleans his upper's study
5:00–7:00	Runs errands and tends his upper's fire
7:00 PM	Tea (bread, butter and tea). Toasts bread for his upper
8:00 PM	'Banco' (rest period). Prayers
9:00 PM	Bed

Silver communion cup, 1630

London maker 'D.W'

One of a pair of communion cups given to the
Charterhouse by John Posten, the first Chapel Clerk.
It is engraved with the hospital's coat of arms and
the initials 'SH', for Sutton's Hospital.

the Governors

The governing arrangements for Sutton's Hospital had been established by Thomas Sutton himself before his death. Ever the businessman, Sutton had taken care to ensure a sound future for his foundation. It was to be run by 16 governors, including a Master who was responsible for daily business. Sutton also secured an Act of Parliament and Letters Patent which gave his hospital legal status as an independent corporation.

The 16 governors of the Charterhouse were always drawn from the great and the powerful. King James I was among the first, along with the Archbishop of Canterbury, and the Lord Chief Justice. All sovereigns of England have been governors of the Charterhouse.

The Charterhouse only lost its royal connections during the Civil War, when a generation of Puritan governors tried to purge the hospital of its royalist and Anglican connections. Oliver Cromwell and Major-General Philip Skippon, London's military governor during 'The Rule of the Major Generals', were both governors, as was John Lisle, the lawyer who had drawn up Charles I's death warrant.

Besides overseeing the institution, early governors looked after the portfolio of property from which Sutton's Hospital derived its main income. Governors also maintained the hospital's scrupulously Protestant character. As the wealthiest charity in Europe, it had to represent the superiority of reformed religion over old Catholic practices. It was 'a masterpiece of Protestant Charity... Peerless in Christiandom'.

Benjamin Laney, Bishop of Ely, c.1670

Oil painting, attributed to Peter Lely (1618–1680)

Benjamin Laney (1591–1675), Bishop of Ely, was made a governor of the Charterhouse in 1668, one of several appointed in the 1660s with the task of restoring Charterhouse's royal connections and Anglican character.

Thomas Sutton

The philanthropist who turned the Charterhouse into the largest charitable foundation in seventeenth-century Europe was Thomas Sutton (1532-1611). A self-made man, Sutton amassed an enormous fortune from property and moneylending. It was said of Sutton, 'it seemed that he only had to sit still and let his money multiply.'

Sutton came from a Lincolnshire gentry family. He had begun his career as the 'well-beloved servant' of the Dudley and Howard families, two powerful aristocratic dynasties in Tudor England. Building up his holdings step by step, by the 1580s Sutton was able to start lending money to his former patrons and other cash-strapped landowners.

Some of Sutton's creditors expected that their debts would be cancelled on his death and their mortgaged lands returned to them. Instead, the terms of his will called in all his loans and charged his executors with distributing his fortune to good causes – chiefly his almshouse and school.

During his lifetime Sutton was known for his wealth and for speculation over who would inherit his fortune (his situation is said to have inspired Ben Jonson's play *Volpone*, first staged in 1606). After Sutton's death his fame grew, but as a role-model for philanthropists. Sutton had put his personal wealth to work for public good, and had done so in a businesslike way: he was seen as an exemplary Protestant figure.

Faith, Hope and Charity overmantel, c.1625

This plaster overmantel was installed in the Master's rooms in the 1620s. The figures represent three virtues: Faith in her armour; Hope with a bird and Charity, the most important of the three for giving life to others.

Portrait of Thomas Sutton, 1677

Engraved by Frederick Hendrik van Hove, (c. 1628–98)

The frontispiece to *Domus Carthusiana: an Account of the Most Noble Foundation of the Charter-House near Smithfield in London...*, by Samuel Herne, 1677. Published 60 years after Sutton's death, Herne's book painted a fulsome picture of Sutton's godliness and generosity.

the Nobles

When Thomas Sutton bought the Charterhouse in 1611 it was one of the great houses of London. Sutton had bought the property for £13,000 from four aristocrats: Thomas Howard, Earl of Suffolk; Theophilus Lord Howard, son and heir of the Earl of Suffolk; Thomas Howard, Earl of Arundel and Surrey; and William Lord Howard of Naworth in Cumberland. All were heirs of the fourth Duke of Norfolk who had owned the Charterhouse between 1565 and 1571.

The transformation into a courtier's house followed from the end of the Charterhouse as a monastery. In the 1540s, the ransacked property was sold to Sir Edward North who turned the ruins into a mansion. It was said that he 'made a Banqueting Hall out of the church'.

The house and its surrounding precinct passed through a succession of aristocratic owners: chiefly Thomas Howard, the fourth Duke of Norfolk, who made it his principal London home. The fourth Duke carried out many improvements and renamed the main building 'Howard House'. Inventories from this time reveal that Howard House was richly furnished with tapestries, paintings, hangings, carpets and upholstered furniture.

As a grand mansion, the Charterhouse was sufficiently splendid to accommodate Royal ceremonies. Elizabeth I and her successor James I both held court here, in the newly created Great Chamber.

King Henry VIII (1491–1547)

Engraving by Peter Vanderbanck (1649–1697)

Henry's dispute with the Catholic Church ended the Charterhouse's existence as a Carthusian monastery. In 1537 the priory's land and buildings were seized by the Crown.

Window pane, painted with the arms of the fourth Duke of Norfolk, 1569

This window pane may well be one of the group noted in a 1588 inventory: '15 escutscheons of glass with arms of Norfolk for glass windows, whereof some are broken'.

OWNERS OF THE CHARTERHOUSE BETWEEN 1537 AND 1611

The owners of the Charterhouse during this tumultuous period were all involved in the political and religious power struggles of Tudor England.

King Henry VIII	1537–1545
Sir Edward North	1545–1553
John Dudley Duke of Northumberland	1553 (executed for treason)
Sir Edward North (Baron North from 1554)	1553–1564
Thomas Howard Fourth Duke of Norfolk	1564–1572 (executed for treason)
Philip Howard Thirteenth Earl of Arundel	1572–1589 (executed for treason, made a Roman Catholic saint in 1970)
Queen Elizabeth I	1589–1601
Thomas Howard Earl of Suffolk	1601–1611

Thomas Howard, Earl of Suffolk (1561–1626)

Painted in 1598, when he was living at the Charterhouse, by permission of the queen.

The Martyrdom of the Carthusian Monks, 1555

Engraving, probably by Nicolas Beatrizet
(fl.1540–1560)

This print was produced in Rome 20 years after
the events depicted. Five of the scenes show
monks from the London Charterhouse imprisoned,
dragged through the streets, hung, drawn and
quartered. The final scene shows the execution
of two Carthusian monks at York. This print was
made at a time when Mary I and her husband
King Philip of Spain were attempting to restore
Catholicism to England.

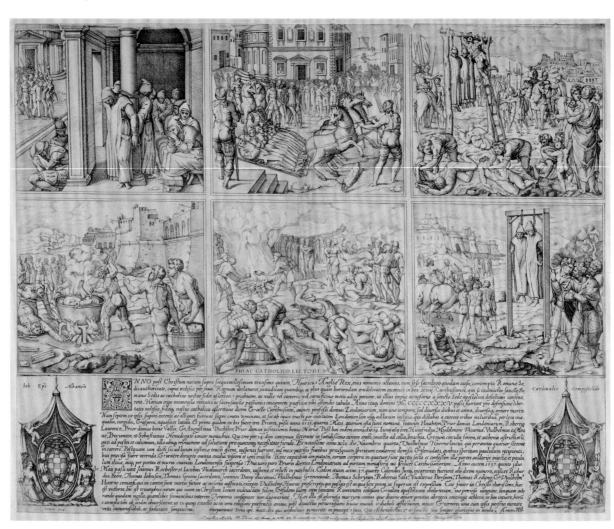

Suppression

Perhaps the most traumatic episode in the Charterhouse's past was the violent end of the monastery. This happened in the 1530s, an inevitable consequence of Henry VIII's suppression of Catholic institutions in favour of his new, Protestant, Church of England.

The Prior who steered the house through the crisis was John Houghton. He was imprisoned in the Tower of London in 1534, released, re-arrested and sentenced to death in April 1535 for refusing to recognise Henry VIII as Head of the Church.

Houghton, two other Carthusian priors, a monk and a lay brother were all executed at Tyburn on 4 May 1535. Houghton's body was chopped into pieces and his arm nailed above the entrance gate at the Charterhouse. Despite this warning, resistance continued. Two years later, a further group of monks and lay-brothers were imprisoned in Newgate and left to starve to death. Others were executed elsewhere. Altogether, 16 men from the London Charterhouse died for their faith.

The last monks quit in 1538, by which time the monastery's property had been seized by the Crown and the main buildings left in ruins.

Sculpture of St Catherine, late 15th century

This is all that remains of a sculpture of St Catherine of Alexandria. She is shown triumphing over the Roman Emperor Maxentius who had ordered her death.

The original sculpture probably stood in the side chapel devoted to St Catherine. When the monastery was sacked, the sculpture was broken up and turned into building stone. This piece had been used to build a wall in Master's Court, from where it was recovered in the 1940s.

'Nunc lege, nunc ora, nunc cum furorie labora
Sic erat hora brevis et labor ille levis'

[Now read, now pray, now work with fervour
Thus the hour will be short and that labour sweet].

Inscription above a monk's cell

the Monks

For more than 160 years after 1371, the Charterhouse was a significant presence in the religious life of London. Not only the largest Carthusian monastery in England, it was also one of the most well endowed, benefiting from its nearness to a large wealthy population.

At its height, the London Charterhouse accommodated around 26 monks, along with up to 40 priests and lay brothers who looked after the daily needs of the holy men. The monks were greatly revered by London's citizens, who gave money and goods to the monastery in return for prayers.

The monks who lived in the Charterhouse were Carthusians. Founded in 1084 by St Bruno, the Carthusian order was especially severe, requiring its members to live in poverty and solitude. The monks' cells were built around a communal cloister, but each lived as a hermit, spending their time in prayer, contemplation and scholarly work, such as copying manuscripts. Carthusians seldom spoke.

Thomas More, later Henry VIII's Lord Chancellor, knew Charterhouse well. Around 1500, uncertain of his vocation, he 'gave himself to devotion and prayer in the Charterhouse of London, religiously lying there without vow about 4 years'. He eventually decided to pursue a life as a lawyer.

Archaeological finds

Fragments of tiles and wall plaster found during archaeological digs on the site of the Great Cloister.

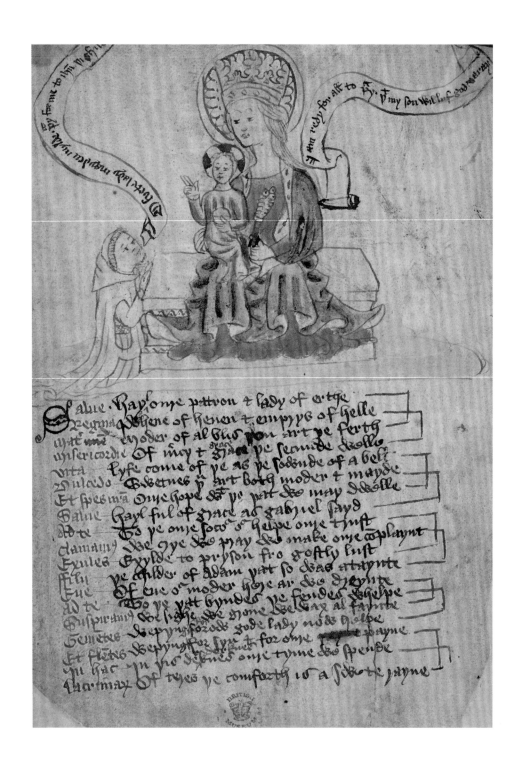

A DAY IN THE LIFE OF A CARTHUSIAN MONK, 1470

3:00 AM	Go to the priory church for *Lauds* or dawn prayers
6:00 AM	*Prime* or early morning prayer in the cell. Walk in the cloister, praying and speaking to no one
9:00 AM	*Terce* or mid-morning prayer in the cell. Solitary work copying manuscripts or reading
MIDDAY	*Sext* or mid-day prayer in the cell. First meal of the day (vegetable soup poured over a slice of bread). Tend the cell's garden or attend to other household tasks
3:00 PM	*None* or mid-afternoon prayer. More solitary work
6:00 PM	Go to the priory church for *Vespers* or evening prayer. Second meal of the day (fish and fruit)
9:00 PM	*Compline* or night prayer, before retiring
MIDNIGHT	*Matins*: prayers in the cell

A Carthusian image of prayer, c.1460–1500

This drawing is part of a manuscript from a charterhouse in northern England. Although not by a London monk, the image echoes the title of the London Charterhouse, The House of the Salutation of the Mother of God. The monk's words are 'Oh sweet lady, maiden mild, pray for me'.

the water system

Sections from a plan of the water system at the Charterhouse, c.1431

This rare manuscript records the water pipes and aqueducts installed in 1431. The system also supplied water to the priory's neighbours and remained functional for many years. A later annotation on the plan refers to the pipes being cleaned in 1511-12.

One of the most fascinating details is the outline of the monastery itself. The 24 monks' cells, each marked with letters of the alphabet, are built around the square of the Great Cloister. In the middle is the conduit – the water tank – housed in a tower.

The water system was installed as a charitable act by Anne Tatersale and William Symmes, a prominent London merchant and member of the Grocers' Company. His donations to the Charterhouse during his lifetime totalled £700 (several £million in today's money). He was a pious man who eventually joined the Carthusians himself, as a novice priest.

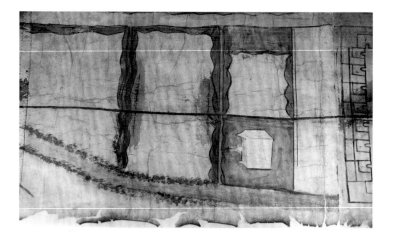

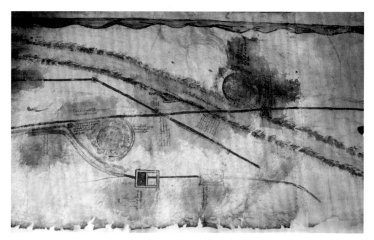

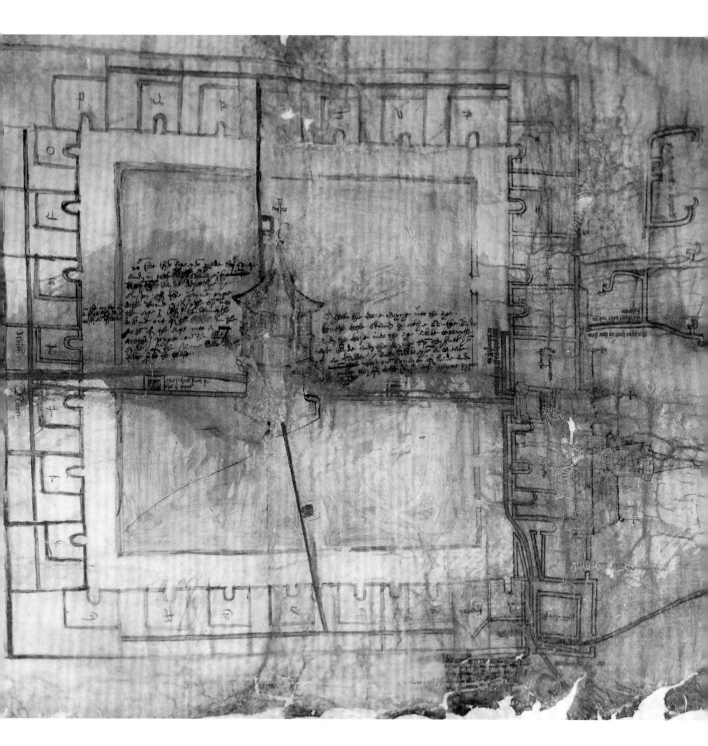

the Dead

Papal Bulla, 1351

This is the lead bulla (seal) of Pope Clement VI. It was recovered from the coffin of Sir Walter Manny in 1947, when his body was exhumed by archaeologists. The bulla was originally attached to a document granting Manny a papal licence to select his own deathbed confessor.

A Carthusian monastery was built on this site as an act of piety. The ground was outside the city walls and had been used to bury many of the Londoners killed by the Black Death, a catastrophic outbreak of plague in 1348-9.

Medieval Christians believed that prayer would enable the souls of the dead to enter heaven. To this end a wealthy courtier and soldier, Sir Walter Manny, built a small chapel at the burial ground. This was the nucleus of the London Charterhouse, which was officially founded in 1371 as 'The House of the Salutation of the Mother of God'.

Over the next 160 years, the Charterhouse became the burial place of choice for many citizens among them Elizabeth Skipworth, whose will (made in 1517) specified that 'my body to be buried in the precinct of the holy place of the Charterhouse, next London'.

The monks and the monastery's patrons were buried inside the priory church and the cloister. The most prestigious spot was reserved for the monastery's principal founder, Sir Walter Manny. He was buried before the high altar in 1372, as requested in his will:

'And my body is to be buried in the Charterhouse, called the house of the Mother of God, outside the walls of London near West Smithfield, which house I founded.'

Fragment from Walter Manny's tomb, 1372

This fragment includes a small shield painted with Sir Walter Manny's coat of arms. Manny's will specified that he was to have an elaborate chest tomb, to include an effigy of himself shown in his knightly armour with his hands joined in prayer, 'in commemoration of me and so that men pray for me'.

A Carthusian image of death, c.1460–1500

This drawing is part of a manuscript from a charterhouse in northern England. It shows a man being speared by the skeleton of death. The monk beside his bed will help the man's soul ascend to heaven, from where Christ watches the earthly scene.

the Black Death

The Black Death was a catastrophe for London. For 18 months in 1348 and 1349, a plague virus swept through the streets, killing swathes of the population and threatening to destroy the city itself.

Emergency burial grounds were opened to cope with the thousands of corpses. Several plots of land to the west of the city's walls were turned into cemeteries, including the ground on which the Charterhouse was subsequently built.

Recent archaeological digs in Charterhouse Square have unearthed several Black Death skeletons which shed new light on this traumatic episode in London's past. One of the unexpected findings was that bodies were buried in layers at different times, suggesting that the Smithfield burial ground was reused when the Black Death returned, as it regularly did after 1348.

Black Death burials in Charterhouse Square

25 skeletons were uncovered in Charterhouse Square in 2013 during construction work for Crossrail. Forensic analysis has dated the skeletons to 1348–50, the period of the Black Death. Traces of DNA from the plague bacterium Yersinia pestis were found in the teeth of some of the skeletons.

the tour of the site

the Chapel Cloister

The exit from the museum room leads into Chapel Cloister. As the name suggests, this space was once a monastic cloister. It was attached to the priory church which was demolished in the 1530s, but whose site is marked on the ground outside, now known as Chapel Court. Looking out, you can see a stone slab marking the site of the tomb of Walter Manny, the priory's founder.

The cloister as you see it today was enclosed in 1614 as part of the building work carried out to adapt the buildings for use as a school and hospital. The splendid doorway leading into the Chapel was carved by Edward Kinsman, a master mason who carried out much of the stonework at this date.

As you enter the Chapel, note the fire-damaged wooden door, a poignant reminder of the inferno that tore through the Charterhouse, causing great damage on the night of 10–11 May 1941 following a direct hit from an incendiary bomb. One of the fire-watchers on duty, Dr Harris of St Bartholomew's Medical College, had the presence of mind to close this door to the Chapel, thus saving the historic woodwork inside.

Chapel Cloister houses many slabs and memorials commemorating former staff, students and Brothers. The large memorial at the west end was set up in 1864 to honour Sir Henry Havelock (an old boy of Charterhouse School) and other Old Carthusians who died during wars in India and the Crimea.

the Chapel

Visitors enter the Chapel through the ante-chapel. The ceiling here provides a rare glimpse of the original monastic fabric: the bosses and moulded stone ribs all date from around 1512. This space was originally a passageway from the Great Cloister to the priory church.

The first aisle in the Chapel was originally the monks' chapterhouse. This was where the community met to discuss matters of common interest, including their defiance of King Henry VIII. When the main church was demolished, the chapterhouse survived and was converted into a small chapel for the use of the owners of the Tudor mansion.

In 1614 the Chapel became an important space for the new hospital, anxious to underline its religious probity. It was extended by adding a second aisle, separated from the original by an arcade of columns. This new aisle accommodated the elaborate monument to Thomas Sutton, but also provided for a newly enlarged congregation of Poor Brothers and Scholars. The richly carved woodwork on the screen, pulpit and organ gallery is all seventeenth century in date, some carried out by master carver John James. An organ was first installed in 1626.

The last extension to the Chapel took place in 1825 when a large bay was added to the north side of the north aisle. This was specifically to accommodate schoolboys who were not Foundation Scholars. Graffiti on the benches testify to their presence (see page 20).

Sutton's Monument

The Chapel is dominated by Thomas Sutton's spectacular monument. Its size and magnificence reflects the desire of Sutton's executors to do justice to the munificence of his charitable bequest. The monument was carved by the partnership of Nicholas Jansen and Edmund Kinsman, London's leading monument-makers. They were joined by Nicholas Stone, an ambitious craftsman who had trained in the Low Countries and brought a sophisticated European feel to his work here. The charge was £400, a sum which also included an additional 'little monument' to John Law, Sutton's executor. This is hung high on the west wall of the south aisle.

Sutton's monument is covered with imagery representing his achievements, his charity and the virtues he embodied. Figures of Faith, Hope and Charity stand on high; two putti and the figures of Peace and Plenty (or Labour and Rest) flank Sutton's coat of arms. A relief panel shows the Poor Brothers in their gowns and a body of pious men and boys (perhaps Scholars) listening to a sermon. The figure blowing bubbles is 'Vanitas', representing the ephemeral quality of worldly pleasure. The figure with a scythe is Time.

Sutton's body lies in a vault beneath his monument.

the Great Hall

THE ENTRANCE HALL

This is the first space visitors encounter in the tour of the Charterhouse's private areas. The present staircase was installed by Seely and Paget in the 1940s, to replace the much grander Jacobean original which was destroyed in the 1941 fire. The 1940s staircase is a plain panelled construction but, like the original, its finials are embellished with Thomas Sutton's greyhound crest.

THE GREAT HALL

The Charterhouse's Tudor character is clearly visible in this splendid space. Constructed by Sir Edward North in the 1540s, the Great Hall was embellished by the Duke of Norfolk around 1571, through the addition of a large carved screen. The ceiling above the original hammer beams was replaced following the destruction of the original by the 1941 fire: scorch marks are still visible at the base of the screen. Apart from that, the Hall is essentially original and constitutes a remarkable and rare survival from Tudor London.

The large chimneypiece was installed in 1614 as part of the works which transformed the Charterhouse into Sutton's Hospital. It was carved by Edmund Kinsman and carries the arms of Thomas Sutton together with emblems of his life and virtue: a salamander in the flames symbolises Constancy and Faith; the small cannon symbolise his service to his country as the one-time Master of Ordnance in Northern Parts for Queen Elizabeth I.

Above the dais is a full-length portrait of Thomas Sutton himself, commissioned by the Governors in 1657. Today the Great Hall is in daily use as the dining hall for the Brothers.

the Screen

The fourth Duke of Norfolk's carved screen is one of Charterhouse's most important treasures. Its rich carving includes the initials 'TH' for Thomas Howard, and the date 1571. The screen is decorated with classical, Renaissance motifs fashionable in the 1570s. It originally had six arches, but the northernmost bay was removed when the long gallery above was inserted, probably in the early seventeenth century.

Tudor visitors would have entered the house through the passage beyond the screen (where the kitchens are now located) and this impressive hall would have been the first room they encountered.

the Library & Cloister

THE OLD LIBRARY

The Old Library is so called because it was the Brothers' Library until 2000. Before that the room was 'Gownboys Hall', the dining-room for the Foundation Scholars. Several Gownboys left their mark on the room, in the form of graffiti carved into the timber columns.

The chimneypiece in this room was installed in 1614 and is by Edmund Kinsman. It bears Thomas Sutton's coat of arms.

THE NORFOLK CLOISTER

The Norfolk Cloister is so called because it was rebuilt by the Duke of Norfolk in 1571 from the ruins of the monk's original Great Cloister. His purpose was entirely secular: at the far end he had built an indoor tennis court, and the cloister provided an arcaded walkway to his new amenity. The roof also served as a pleasant promenade, along which Norfolk and his guests, including Queen Elizabeth I, could stroll and admire the gardens. The Norfolk Cloister is thus 'a rare survival of a great Elizabethan garden gallery'.

The Norfolk Cloister was originally double the length you now see. In its full length it formed one side of the Great Cloister's square of monastic cells built around open ground. Five or seven cells opened off each side of the square. The door to Cell B can still be seen here. The small opening to the left of the door is for passing food to the resident monk without disturbing his solitude.

With the arrival of Sutton's Hospital, the cloister area, including Norfolk's tennis court, was assigned to the school. The open space at the centre of the cloister became 'Upper Green', the grounds used for cricket, athletics and school photographs. The Norfolk Cloister was pressed into use for football, its narrow dimensions creating the need for the offside rule.

This section of the Norfolk Cloister is the only remnant of the monastic cloister still attached to the Charterhouse. When Merchant Taylors'

School bought the school grounds in the 1870s, the Norfolk Cloister was cut in half, in order to build a new assembly hall at its northern end. This has since been demolished. The buildings now seen through the Norfolk Cloister's windows belong to the current owner of the site, Barts and The London School of Medicine and Dentistry.

THE MONK'S GARDEN

At the end of the Norfolk Cloister, visitors can enter a small garden planted to evoke the world of the medieval monk. Carthusian cells were in effect two-storey cottages, with a small cottage garden attached. The monks were vegetarian so garden produce would have been important to their diet. Archaeological digs on the site of the Great Cloister have unearthed pips and seeds from a wide range of edible plants.

the Great Chamber

This is the Charterhouse's most splendid room, described at various times in its history as 'The Throne Room', 'The Gilded Room', The Tapestry Room' and 'The Governors' Room'. The room was constructed by Lord North, but much embellished by the Duke of Norfolk, whose arms appear on the plaster ceiling together with his family motto *Sola Virtus Invicta* (courage alone is invincible).

The ceiling was much damaged during the 1941 fire, but the section in the far alcove is entirely original. Intriguingly, the decoration includes a thistle emblem that could be read as revealing Norfolk's admiration for Mary, Queen of Scots. His association with Mary led to his eventual execution in 1572.

This room has seen several royal occasions. Elizabeth I held court here in November 1558, on the eve of her formal entry into the City of London as queen. In similar fashion, King James I (the son of Mary, Queen of Scots) gathered his courtiers here in May 1603 before entering London as king. Charterhouse was then owned by Thomas Howard, Earl of Suffolk, son of the fourth Duke of Norfolk.

During the hospital era, the governors held their meetings in this room. In 1784 the antechamber (formerly the eastern end of the room) was turned into a library for the collection of rare books given by the widow of Daniel Wray, an old boy of Charterhouse School. The room's present dimensions date from the post-war rebuilding.

The elaborate painted chimneypiece at the west end of the Great Chamber was probably installed by the fourth Duke of Norfolk. Exactly what it looked like in Norfolk's day is difficult to judge as it has since been much altered. As you see it today, it bears Sutton's coat of arms and the Stuart arms. The former was added in 1624-6 when a painter Rowland Buckett was paid £50 by the Governors for various works including 'painting and gilding the chimneypiece'.

The painted scenes depict the Annunciation, the Last Supper, figures of the four Evangelists and figures of Peace and Plenty. The Last Supper scene was painted on canvas and then attached in the 1950s when the chimneypiece was restored after fire damage.

It has been speculated that the four faces of children on the top cornice show the Duke of Norfolk's three sons and his stepson. But these are also 1950s replacements for the originals which were burnt in the Blitz.

Graffiti

Some former residents or visitors left their mark on the Great Chamber in the form of graffiti scratched into the glass window panes.

Master's Court

Master's Court is so called because the Master of Charterhouse used to live in the south range, occupying the space that formed the mansion's long gallery in Tudor times.

This has always been the most important of Charterhouse's courtyards. It was constructed by Lord North to provide a theatrical entrance to his mansion, making the most of the effect created by the large windows of his Great Hall. The visual drama was enhanced by the governors of Sutton's Hospital who added an entrance porch and sundial in 1628. The eye-catching Royal coat of arms was erected in 1660 to celebrate the restoration of Charles II.

This was originally the site of the monks' Little Cloister which adjoined the south and west corners of the priory church: strips of white stone in the paving mark the outline. The walls of the north and east ranges include the odd piece of carved or dressed stone, a reminder that North built his mansion from the ruins of the monastery and used the stone available on site. The statue of St Catherine (p. 31) was recovered from a wall in Master's Court.

Wash-house Court

This is the oldest of the Charterhouse's courtyards. Originally the service area of the priory, its buildings survived most of the subsequent changes of ownership. As the name suggests, this was in effect the servants' quarters, where clothes were laundered and pots were cleaned. Wash-house Court also survived the 1941 fire.

The stone-built range on the north side may include parts of the original monastery buildings. The brick-built ranges on the west and south sides were probably completed in the 1530s only just before the priory was shut down. The timber-framing beneath the brick is partially exposed in the small passageway in the north-west corner.

Passing through the passage, note the outer, west-facing front, with its distinctive decorative brickwork. The meaning of the diapers, diamonds, crosses and the initials 'IH' is much speculated on. Some believe that IH stands for John Houghton, the last prior: others, that the initials were originally IHS, a well-known Catholic cypher.

Private Courtyards

The Charterhouse's other courtyards cannot normally be visited. They are private areas for the Brothers and other residents.

PREACHER'S COURT

North of Wash-house Court, this courtyard embraces Charterhouse's most modern addition, the Admiral Ashmore building opened in 2000 and designed by Michael Hopkins & Partners.

PENSIONERS' COURT

This was built in the 1820s and 1830s to provide better accommodation for the Brothers. However, the Brothers now live in the main building and the Admiral Ashmore building. The properties here are now let commercially as flats and offices.

ENTRANCE COURT

The area south of Wash-house Court incorporates the medieval arch into the monks' inner precinct. From here, the old pedestrian entrance route leads through to Master's Court beneath a gilded plaque with Sutton's coat of arms and the date 1611, the founding date of Sutton's Hospital.

THE GARDENS

The Charterhouse's gardens are greatly valued by those who live and work here. The gardens are looked after with skill and imagination by a Head Gardener and her team (which includes volunteers). Among the most venerable plants in the garden are the mulberry trees in Preacher's Court. The first mulberry pickings are presented to the Lord Mayor of London every summer as a continuing Charterhouse tradition.

Charterhouse Square

Charterhouse Square was originally open ground outside the walls of the City of London. The land was enclosed in 1348 to form a burial ground for victims of the Black Death. Since then, the land has never been built on – apart from a small chapel, demolished around 1615, and the monks' 'flesh' kitchen (for preparing meat for visitors).

What was originally known as Charterhouse Yard formed the outer precinct of the Carthusian monastery. Thereafter, ownership became more fragmented with several aristocratic houses built in separate plots around the edges. By the late seventeenth century, Charterhouse Yard was taking on the character of a residential London square. In the 1740s an Act of Parliament allowed the residents to raise local rates to finance its upkeep.

The Square remained relatively secluded until the 1870s when a new road was driven through its south side, joining the newly built Smithfield Market with Aldersgate, the main road north. The iron gates that stand at the south and west entrances to the Square were installed at this time to protect the Square from the increased traffic.

The rebuilding of Smithfield Market, together with the arrival of the new underground railway, gave the Square a more commercial and industrial character that it kept until the late twentieth century, when the area became quieter.

THE NORTH SIDE

Today, the north side of the Square is dominated by the Charterhouse, with its old and new entrances on either side of the medieval chequerboard wall.

The Charterhouse's new entrance railings and gates were installed in 2016. Designed by Eric Parry Architects, the wrought iron structures celebrate the craft of blacksmithing. The lettering along the top of the railings spells out the Latin mottos of some former owners of the Charterhouse.

Honi Soit Qui Mal Y Pense (shame on him who thinks evil)
Sir Walter Manny (1310–1372)

La Vertu Est La Seule Noblesse (virtue is the only nobility)
Edward, first Baron North (1496–1564)

Sola Virtus Invicta (courage alone is invincible)
Thomas Howard, fourth Duke of Norfolk (1536–1572)

Deo Dante Dedi (because God has given, I give)
Thomas Sutton (1532–1611)

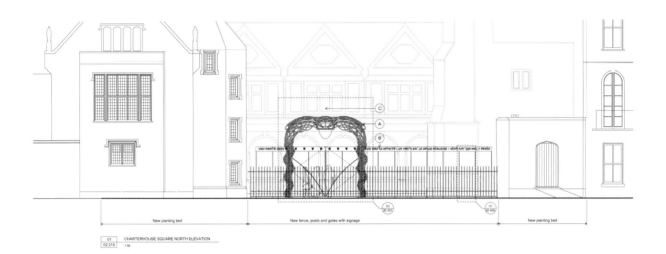

New planting bed	New fence, posts and gates with signage

New planting bed

01	CHARTERHOUSE SQUARE NORTH ELEVATION
02 210	1:50

THE EAST SIDE

The east side of Charterhouse Square is
dominated by Florin Court, a stylish block of flats
built in the 1930s for use by businessmen. The
block, which originally included a restaurant,
cocktail bar and roof garden, is often used as a
film set for 1930s period dramas.

The group of terraced houses adjoining
Florin Court to the south are the Square's oldest
domestic buildings. All were built just before 1700
as smart town houses for the gentry or wealthy
professionals.

the Gardens

From 2016 the central gardens in Charterhouse Square will be open to the public during the Charterhouse's opening hours (11:00 – 5:00, Tuesday to Saturday). This is a significant change. The Square's gardens were enclosed in the eighteenth century and since then have remained largely inaccessible to all but key-holding residents.

The opening-up of the Square has been accompanied by an extensive refurbishment and replanting by Todd Longstaffe-Gowan, landscape architect and expert in London's historic garden squares. Three new entrances have been created and the early eighteenth-century layout of two diagonal pathways has been reinstated.

The new planting scheme aims to be horticulturally rich so as to increase the biodiversity value of the half-hectare space. Parts of the grassed area have been set aside as a wild-flower meadow. The perimeter hedge is now made up of traditional English hedging plants – including hawthorn, blackthorn, holly, common privet, hazel, rowan and guilder rose. Altogether, the new Square will provide a better habitat for birds and insects as well as for people.

At night the Square's gardens will be almost entirely lit by gas lamps. During the day, the gardens will be managed by the Charterhouse's full-time gardener with her team of volunteers and garden apprentices.

THE PAVILION

The small pavilion in the south-east corner of the gardens has been built as an eye-catcher to mark the start of the Charterhouse precinct. The pavilion is designed to be 'a garden cabinet – in the spirit of the late seventeenth century – which serves as both a shady retreat and place in which to provide some interpretative material'. The latter includes an ornamental mosaic floor emblazoned with coats of arms associated with the Charterhouse.

Charterhouse Square, 1816 and 2016

The top view is an artist's impression of the Square following the 2016 replanting. The bottom view is a hand-coloured print published in 1816 showing a corner of the Square gardens at a time when they were not accessible to the public.

Visitor Information

OPENING HOURS

11:00–5:00 Tuesday to Sunday. Last entry: **4:45**
Admission to the museum and Chapel is free.
This does not include a tour of the historic interiors, which has to be booked.

TOURS

Guided tours run every day during opening hours. Please ask at Reception for further information.

ACCESS AND FACILITIES FOR VISITORS WITH DISABILITIES

The museum room, the Sir John Cass's Foundation Learning Room and the Chapel are fully accessible to wheelchair users. Areas visited on the tours are generally accessible, but there are some stairs to negotiate. Wheelchair users wishing to go on a tour should get in touch in advance so that we can discuss how best to help.

THE SIR JOHN CASS'S FOUNDATION LEARNING CENTRE

The Sir John Cass's Foundation Learning Room is a new and well-equipped space at the Charterhouse designed for use by schools. We offer a full programme of schools sessions, and learning activities for families and other groups. All are run in collaboration with the Museum of London.
For details see: www.thecharterhouse.org
and www.museumoflondon.org.uk/learning

To discuss a school visit please contact our Learning Manager on 0207 253 9503

FOR GROUP VISITS

We can offer a lively selection of tours, talks and walks tailored to the particular needs of your group. To discuss, please contact our Visitor Services Manager on 0207 253 9503

SHOP

The Charterhouse has a small shop, stocking books, souvenirs and gifts.

EATING AND DRINKING

The Charterhouse café is located next to the public entrance at 13–14 Charterhouse Square. There are many other cafés and restaurants in the area.

FOR GENERAL INFORMATION

Telephone 020 7253 9503 or visit
www.thecharterhouse.org

BECOMING A BROTHER

Please see our website. Vacancies are advertised as they arise.

LOCATION

The Charterhouse is in West Smithfield.

Nearest tube stations: Barbican and Farringdon.

Nearest rail station: Farringdon Thameslink and [from 2018] Farringdon Crossrail.

Nearest bus stops: in Aldersgate Street (routes 4, 56, 153); in Clerkenwell Road (routes 53, 55, 243)

the Charterhouse

Charterhouse Square, London EC1M 6AN

www.thecharterhouse.org